LAWS, BY-LAWS,

AND

RULES AND REGULATIONS

OF THE

REFORM SCHOOL

OF THE

DISTRICT OF COLUMBIA.

1880.

———◆———

WASHINGTON:
GOVERNMENT PRINTING OFFICE.
1880.

OFFICE OF BOARD OF TRUSTEES,
REFORM SCHOOL, DISTRICT OF COLUMBIA,
Washington, D. C., October 15, 1877.

The following by-laws, rules, and regulations were this day adopted for the government of the Reform School of the District of Columbia, and will remain in full force and effect until altered, amended, or repealed.

By order of the board of trustees.

N. W. BURCHELL,
President of the Board.

WM. B. PEDDRICK,
Secretary.

Approved.

CHAS. DEVENS,
Attorney-General, United States. .

BY-LAWS AND RULES AND REGULATIONS FOR THE REFORM SCHOOL OF THE DISTRICT OF COLUMBIA.

CHAPTER I.

ITS OBJECT, AND THE MEANS TO ACCOMPLISH IT.

SECTION 1. The Reform School is established for one purpose, to wit, the reformation of the inmates detained therein.

SEC. 2. The means to be employed are instruction and labor, under thorough discipline, accompanied by rewards and punishments, as may be deserved by the inmates.

SEC. 3. The instruction will embrace mental and physical culture, teaching and preparing the inmates, while in the institution, how to live after they leave it.

SEC. 4. The labor shall be such as suits the capacity and age of the inmates, respectively; it shall not be imposed as a punishment. The inmates shall be made to feel that they are taught to labor so that they may acquire regular habits, a love of industry, and aversion to idleness, and thus be fitted to gain a livelihood when they shall go out into the world.

SEC. 5. The discipline shall be that of the family, the school, the work-shop, and the farm, and not of a prison. The inmates are to be watched over and treated as pupils and not guarded as prisoners or criminals, and there shall be no more restraint than shall be necessary to develop in them good and repress bad qualities. Self-instruction, self-desire to labor, and self-government shall be inculcated as the best culture as well as the most effective discipline.

SEC. 6. Every effort of the inmates toward self-improvement shall be encouraged and suitably rewarded.

CHAPTER II.

THE GOVERNMENT.

SECTION 1. The board of trustees, including the consulting members, shall exercise a frequent and wholesome supervision over the school, and see that its objects and purposes are properly carried out. They shall hold regular meetings on the last Monday of every month, at the institution; but special meetings may be called by the president at any time and at any place, or upon the request of two members it shall be obligatory upon him to do so.

Officers.

SEC. 2. The election of president, vice-president, secretary, and treasurer shall be held at the regular meeting in December in each year.

SEC. 3. In the absence of the president and vice-president, the board shall designate some other member who shall act as president *pro tempore.*

Secretary.

SEC. 4. The secretary shall keep an accurate record of the proceedings in a book to be provided for that purpose, and shall give written notice to each trustee of the time and place of all meetings of the board.

Treasurer.

SEC. 5. The treasurer shall perform such duties as are defined by acts of Congress.

SEC. 6. At the regular meeting held in the month of September in each year the annual report of the superintendent and that of the board, the latter to be prepared by the president, shall be submitted for approval and transmission to the Attorney-General of the United States.

SEC. 7. Nominations and elections of officers for the Reform School shall be made by the board of trustees on the report of the executive committee. The superintendent may, with the advice and consent of said executive committee, temporarily appoint officers or assistants when their services are needed, but such appointments shall continue only until the next meeting of the board.

SEC. 8. Removals or dismissals of officers or assistants shall be made by the board upon the recommendation of the executive committee, but before any removals are made the person or persons subject to such removal may be heard before the committee in their defense if they so desire. The superintendent shall have power, however, to suspend any employé, for good reasons, where circumstances admit of no delay, until the matter can be laid before said committee.

Committees.

SEC. 9. There shall be an executive, a building, and a finance committee, to be appointed by the president of the board, of the first of which the president shall be chairman.

SEC. 10 It shall be the duty of the executive committee to attend to all matters relating to the government and operations of the school, and, in concert with the superintendent, provide for variously employing the boys in farming, gardening, and mechanical industries. They shall also advise and act with the superintendent in purchasing and disposing of any live stock, horses, wagons, carriages, and of materials to be worked by the boys, as well as other products of their labor. All matters not properly belonging to the building or finance committees shall fall under the charge of this committee.

SEC. 11. It shall be the duty of the building committee to supervise the erection of buildings, repairs, and alterations; to attend to the purchase of all necessary materials, in concert with such officers as may be duly authorized; to approve bills for materials and the pay-rolls for labor performed, which shall be, in the hands of the treasurer, a voucher for the payment of the same; and they shall generally give such attention and do such acts in reference to building, repairing, and removing buildings as may be required for the welfare of the school.

SEC. 12. It shall be the duty of the finance committee to examine accounts made in the purchase of supplies, fuel, clothing, &c., for the institution monthly, and, if found correct, to approve the same.

They shall also examine the pay-rolls for the salaries of the officers and employés, at the same time, and when a list of purchases on the pay-poll shall have been approved by a majority of said committee, it shall be, in the hands of the treasurer, a voucher for payment. All bills contracted, other than those referred to in this and the preceding section, shall be brought before the board, and, if passed, shall be approved by a majority of the committee and paid by the treasurer.

They shall approve all bills against the District Government for support of inmates, and all other bills *due* the institution, and make requisitions for the money, payable to the treasurer of the board.

The superintendent shall report monthly all money received by him from any source, and pay the same over to the treasurer of the board.

CHAPTER III.

DUTIES OF OFFICERS.

SECTION 1. The superintendent shall reside at the Reform School, and shall devote all his time to the interests of the institutoin. He shall be the superior officer of the school; he shall have the general charge of the inmates and business of the institution, and shall present to the board, at each regular meeting, a clear record of the business transacted during the month.

He shall see that the officers and assistants are punctual and faithful in the discharge of their respective duties, and that the regulations and by-laws are carefully observed and carried out. He shall also keep accurate and detailed accounts of all purchases made by him, moneys paid out, articles sold, and moneys received, which accounts shall be rendered monthly to the finance committee. He shall also make such reports as are required by the seventh section of the act of Congress approved May 3, 1876.

SEC. 2. The assistant superintendent shall have charge of a family, and in the absence of the superintendent shall be the officer in charge.

SEC. 3. The teacher or assistants and master-mechanics shall be called elder brothers, and there shall be two such officers for each family. The gardner, farmer, servants, and laborers shall perform such duties as the superintendent may direct.

SEC. 4. Resignations of any officers or assistants at the institution shall be tendered in writing, and shall not take effect until thirty days after being presented, except with the consent of the board or executive committee. Should any officer or assistant leave abruptly, and without such consent, the same shall forfeit any compensation due him at such time.

SEC. 5. It shall be the duty of the officers and assistants to remain constantly at the institution, unless leave of absence is granted by the superintendent. Subordinate officers, in addition to their specific duties, shall aid the superintendent in preserving order and quiet among the inmates, in guarding against escapes, and generally maintaining the rules and discipline of the institution. They shall also perform such other service, from time to time, as the superintendent may require.

SEC. 6. One or both of the elder brothers must be present with the boys at all times, and have charge of them in all things; they shall instruct them in such branches of education as may be directed by the board of trustees, and in the arrangement and classification of students shall follow the general direction of the superintendent; they shall strive to inspire the boys with a love of study, and lead them justly to estimate the value of a sound practical education, and shall make an effort, by precept and example, to impress upon their minds the importance of good order, self-government, and purity of body and mind.

They shall attend to the cleanliness of the school-rooms, dormitories, yards, &c., and shall be responsible for the safety, care, and preservation of all books and furniture belonging to their respective rooms or buildings, and, by strict personal examination, see that no injury or waste is suffered. They shall teach the boys proper manners for the table, good order for the dormitory, and politeness toward each other. Each elder brother shall pass to the table with his class at all meals, to see that the boys are properly seated and their necessary wants supplied.

One or more officers shall remain in the dining-room during meals, that perfect order may be maintained. Slovenly or hasty eating must not be allowed, and the boys must be polite and mannerly in their deportment. Any violation of the rules of strict propriety at the table must receive the immediate attention of the officer in charge.

The elder brothers shall lead the boys in saying grace before each meal, and shall also take charge of the morning and evening devotions.

They shall spend a portion of each evening in moral review of their respective families, at which time a record of the conduct of each youth shall be made in a book kept for that purpose. This book shall be the basis upon which the standing of every boy shall be determined.

The elder brothers shall go to the field with their respective classes, to perform such work as may be designated by the superintendent. The work shall be so arranged, if possible, that all the boys will get a practical knowledge of farming and gardening.

SEC. 7. The matron shall have the general charge and supervision of all the domestic arrangements of the institution. The sewing-rooms, laundry, and hospital shall be conducted under her direction, and she shall see that cleanliness, order, and propriety are maintained in these departments. She shall see that all female assistants are diligent and faithful in the discharge of their appropriate duties, discreet in their deportment, and strict in the observance of all the rules of the institution, and shall report to the superintendent any remissness that may come to her knowledge. She shall see that the sick receive proper attention, and shall have a maternal regard for the health and physical welfare of all the boys. She shall see that there is no unnecessary waste in the kitchen department, and that a sufficient quantity of clean and well-cooked food is furnished for the tables at each meal and served in a careful manner. She shall also see that the clothing of the boys is kept in a tidy and neat condition.

SEC. 8. The night-watchmen shall watch over the boys from the time they retire until they rise in the morning. At half-past five a. m. they shall cause the boys to rise, make their beds neatly, wash, and prepare for breakfast. Any case of disorderly conduct or sickness during the night shall be immediately reported to the superintendent.

They shall perform a regular patrol through and around the buildings during the night, in which they shall exercise due vigilance to prevent misconduct, and to discover and prevent danger from fire. They shall perform any other duties assigned them by the superintendent.

CHAPTER IV.

GENERAL REGULATIONS.

SECTION 1. Punishment shall be imposed as a public judgment, and *never* under the excitement of the moment. It may be inflicted by the deprivation of amusements or recreation; by withholding some favorite article of food, or by substituting bread and water for the regular meal; by loss of rank or standing in the class; by the performance of some irksome duty; by solitary confinemen' for a limited period, or, in extreme cases, by the infliction of moderate corporal punishment.

In all cases care should be taken to impress the delinquents with the conviction that the object in administering punishment is to subdue their vicious passions, to promote their welfare individually, and to secure the good of the institution, and at the same time to convince them beyond a doubt that discipline and good order will be maintained at all hazards. For all minor offenses and indiscretions gentle admonition and reproof should be adopted; but any officer or assistant having charge of boys, may use all judicious force necessary to repress any violent or obstinate and persistent resistance to his orders, and in all such cases the offender shall be confined in the lock-up, or otherwise secured, and the fact reported to the superintendent, who shall cause to be kept a record of all corporal punishments and cases of solitary confinement, and submit the same to the board at each regular meeting.

SEC. 2. In cases of attempt at escape, it shall be the duty of all employed in the institution to follow at once in the pursuit of the fugitive or fugitives, under the direction of the superintendent, and to assist in the arrest of the same, and they shall have full power to use any and all proper means necessary to retake him or them.

Should recapture fail, then the superintendent shall place the proper process in the hands of some constable or police officer, and offer a suitable reward, not to exceed $25, for the capture of the boy.

Any attempt to escape shall wipe out all merit-marks due such fugitive, and he shall, when recaptured, be degraded to class eight, and he shall also be liable to such punishment as the superintendent, with the advice of the elder brothers, may inflict, which may extend to solitary confinement for two weeks in the lock up.

SEC. 3. When a boy shall be discharged upon having gained his honors, he shall be entitled to, and receive, if the board so orders, from the superintendent, a new suit of clothes, hat, and shoes, and a sum not to exceed $10, and shall give to the superintendent a receipt for the money, which shall be the superintendent's voucher to the treasurer for the payment thereof.

SEC. 4. Visitors shall at all reasonable hours be welcome to the

Reform School, under such regulations as the board may prescribe, and on such days as the board may direct.

No spirituous or intoxicating drinks shall be brought to the institution, except for medicinal purposes. No officer shall at any time make use of such liquors unless ordered by a physician.

There shall be no smoking, even by visitors, in or about the school.

The clothing of the inmates shall be comfortable, according to the season, and shall be well made and mended as often as needed.

No person regularly employed shall be absent from his duties without permission from the superintendent. All persons employed at the institution shall attend to the daily devotional exercises when practicable; shall also attend all religious exercises on the Sabbath, unless special leave of absence is granted.

All officers shall strive to carry out the spirit, as well as the letter of the regulations of the institution, and hold themselves in readiness at all times for any emergency, and by general and constant acts of accommodation, firmness, and kindness aid in advancing the reformation of the boys.

Discharged boys, or parents or friends of the inmates of the institution will be permitted to visit the boys once a month, and between the hours of 12 m. and 3 p. m., except on Sundays.

CHAPTER V.

ORDER OF BUSINESS.

1. Reading the minutes of the last meeting, the trustees and secretary of the board alone being present.
2. Reading reports of committees.
3. Receiving the report of the superintendent and taking action on all matters requiring his presence.
4. New business.

These by-laws may be altered, amended, or repealed at any regular meeting of the board.

[PUBLIC—No. 54.]

AN ACT revising and amending the various acts establishing and relating to the Reform School in the District of Columbia.

Be it enacted by the Senate and House of Representatives of the United States of America in Congress assembled, That the institution known as the Reform School of the District of Columbia shall be in the charge of, and governed and managed by, a board of seven trustees, who shall be appointed by the President of the United States, upon the recommendation of the Attorney-General, each for the term of three years, but in such a manner that the terms of not more than three of them shall expire within any one or the same year; that one of the trustees shall be elected president of the board, whose duty shall be prescribed by the board.

SEC. 2. That the board of trustees shall be a corporation by the name of the "Board of Trustees of the Reform School of the District of Columbia," for the purpose of taking and holding in trust, for the United States, property of every description which has been purchased, appropriated, or set apart for the use of the institution, or which may hereafter be purchased, appropriated, or set apart for its use, or given or bequeathed to it, or to the said board, for its use, with all power necessary to carry this purpose into effect, and to protect and preserve such property, including the land and buildings, fences, stock, fruit, crops, and trees of all kinds.

SEC. 3. That the board of trustees may appoint a superintendent, two or more teachers or assistants, and a matron, whose salaries are fixed by law; they may also employ two or more master mechanics, a farmer, a gardener, and such other persons, as servants and laborers, as may be necessary, and fix their compensation, subject to the approval of the Attorney-General.

SEC. 4. That the board of trustees shall appoint a treasurer, who shall, before entering upon the duties of his office, give a bond to the United States with two or more sureties, to be approved by the First Comptroller of the Treasury, in the sum of twenty thousand dollars, or a larger sum, at the option of the said Comptroller, conditioned that he shall faithfully account for all the money received by him as treasurer; and it shall be his duty to keep a clear and full record of his accounts as treasurer, and report an abstract of the same to the board of trustees once in every two months, and shall also make an annual report to the board of trustees.

SEC. 5. That before entering upon the duties of his office, the superintendent shall give a bond to the board of trustees, with sureties, to be approved by the Attorney-General of the United States, in the sum of three thousand dollars, conditioned that he shall faithfully account for all money received by him, and faithfully perform all the duties incumbent on him as superintendent of said Reform School.

SEC. 6. That the superintendent shall reside at the institution constantly, and that he, with such subordinate officers as may be appointed in accordance with the third section of this act, shall have the charge and custody of the boys; shall govern them in accordance with such rules and regulations as the board of trustees may prescribe in its by-laws; shall employ them in agricultural, mechanical, or other labor; shall give them instruction in reading, writing, arithmetic, geography, and such other studies and in such arts and trades as the trustees may direct; and shall employ such methods of discipline as will, as far as possible, reform their characters, preserve their health, promote regular improvement in their studies and employments, and secure in them fixed habits of religion, morality, and industry.

SEC. 7. That the superintendent shall have charge of the lands, buildings, furniture, tools, implements, stock, provisions, and every other species of property pertaining to the institution, within the precincts thereof, under the board of trustees, including the farm in possession of the board where the school was first located; and he shall keep, in suitable books, regular and complete accounts of all his receipts and expenditures, and of all the property intrusted to him, so as to show clearly the income and expenses of the institution; and he shall account, in such manner as the trustees may prescribe, for all the money received by him from the proceeds of the institution or otherwise; and he shall keep a register of the names and ages of all boys committed to the institution, with the dates of their admission and discharge, and such particulars of the history before and after leaving the institution as he can obtain.

His books, and all documents relating to the Reform School, shall, at all times, be open to the inspection of the trustees, who shall, once or more in every month, carefully examine his accounts, and the vouchers and documents connected therewith, and make a record of the result of such examination; and once in every three months the institution shall be thoroughly examined in all its departments by three or more of the trustees, and a report of such examination shall be made to the board.

SEC. 8. That whenever any boy under the age of sixteen years shall be brought before any court of the District of Columbia, or any judge of such court, and shall be convicted of any crime or misdemeanor punishable by fine or imprisonment, other than imprisonment for life, such court or judge, in lieu of sentencing him to imprisonment in the county jail or fining him, may commit him to the Reform School, to remain until he shall arrive at the age of twenty-one years, unless sooner discharged by the board of trustees. And the judges of the criminal and police courts of the District of Columbia shall have power to commit to the Reform School, first, any boy under sixteen years of age who may be liable to punishment by imprisonment under any existing law of the District of Columbia, or any law that may be enacted and in force in said District; second, any boy under sixteen years of age, with the consent of his parent or guardian, against whom any charge of committing any crime or misdemeanor shall have been made, the punishment of which, on conviction, would be confinement in jail or prison; third, any boy under sixteen years of age who is destitute of a suitable home and adequate means of obtaining an honest living, or who is in danger of being brought up, or is brought up, to lead an idle or vicious life; fourth, any boy under sixteen years of age who is incorrigible, or habitually disregards the commands of his father or mother or guardian, who leads a vagrant life, or resorts to immoral places or practices, or neglects or refuses to perform labor suitable to his years and condition, or to attend school. And the president of the board of trustees may also commit to the Reform School such boys as are mentioned in the foregoing third and fourth classes upon application or complaint, in writing, of a parent or guardian, or relative having charge of such boy, and upon such testimony in regard to the facts stated as shall be satisfactory to him; and for taking testimony in such cases he is hereby empowered to administer oaths.

SEC. 9. That every boy sent to the Reform School shall remain until he is twenty-one years of age, unless sooner discharged or bound as an apprentice; but no boy shall be retained after the superintendent shall have reported him fully reformed.

SEC. 10. That whenever there shall be as large a number of boys in the school as can be properly accommodated, it shall be the duty of the president of the board of trustees to give notice to the criminal and police courts of the fact; whereupon no boys shall be sent to the school by the said courts until notice shall be given them by the president of the board that more can be received.

SEC. 11. That if any person shall entice, or attempt to entice, away from said school any boy legally committed to the same, or shall harbor, conceal, or aid in harboring or concealing any boy who shall have escaped from said school, such person shall, upon conviction thereof, be deemed guilty of a misdemeanor, and shall pay a fine of not less than ten nor more than one hundred dollars, which shall be paid to the treasurer of the board of trustees; and any policeman shall have power, and it is hereby made his duty, to arrest any boy, when in his power so to do, who shall have escaped from said school, and return him thereto.

SEC. 12. That the trustees shall have full power to place any boy committed as herein described, during his minority, at such employment, and cause him to be instructed in such branches of useful knowledge, as may be suitable to his years and capacity, as they may see fit; and they may, with the consent of any such boy, bind him out as an apprentice during his minority, or for a shorter period, to learn such trade and employment as in their judgment will tend to his future benefit; and the president of the board shall, for such purpose, have power to execute and deliver, on behalf of the said board, indentures of apprenticeship for any such boy; and such indentures shall have the same force and effect as other indentures of apprenticeship under the laws of the District of Columbia, and be filed and kept among the records in the office of the Reform School, and it shall not be necessary to record or file them elsewhere.

SEC. 13. That for the support of the boys sent to the Reform School, as hereinbefore mentioned, the District of Columbia shall pay to the board of trustees two dollars for each boy per week; and it shall be the duty of the superintendent to make out and render to the proper officers monthly accounts at the close of each month for the support of the boys in said school, which shall be paid on demand; and, if not paid within ten days from the time the account is presented, shall draw interest at the rate of one per centum per month until paid.

SEC. 14. That all contracts and purchases made for or on account of the institution shall be made in the name of the board and by whomsoever the board may direct. The president of the board shall be its executive officer, and it shall be his duty to make an annual report to the Attorney-General, to be accompanied by the annual report of the superintendent and treasurer.

SEC. 15. That the board of trustees may make such by-laws, rules, and regulations for their own and the government of the institution, its officers, employés, and inmates, as they may deem necessary and proper.

SEC. 16. That two consulting trustees shall be appointed, namely, one Senator of the United States, by the presiding officer of the Senate, for the term of four years, and one member of the House of Representatives, by the Speaker thereof, for the terms of two years.

SEC. 17. That all acts and parts of acts incompatible with this act are hereby repealed.

Approved, May 3, 1876.

2

THE REFORM SCHOOL OF THE DISTRICT OF COLUMBIA.

This institution was created by act of Congress approved 25th of July, 1866, under the title of the "House of Correction," which grew out of a former one designated as "The Guardian Society," incorporated by act of Congress approved July 1, 1862. The latter society raised some five or six thousand dollars, through the liberality of a few citizens and banking institutions of Washington, obtained a large building in 1865, erected near the city as a hospital during the rebellion, and removed it to the "Government Farm," situated about half a mile from the Potomac River, four miles northwest from Georgetown; but their funds being exhausted, the act first mentioned was passed, incorporating the trustees of the House of Correction, and appropriating $12,000 for the benefit of the institution. This, however, only sufficed to prepare the building for the reception of the boys, leaving no adequate funds to carry on the institution.

Although the board of directors were unable to put the institution into satisfactory operation, it was, however, deemed advisable to organize the school by appointing a superintendent and receiving a small number of boys, sent to the institution by the criminal court, relying upon Congress to make such appropriation as would enable them to carry it on; and the first boys, two in number, were admitted January 13, 1870.

The location of the school upon the Government Farm, on the Potomac River, having unfortunately proved unhealthy during the summer and fall of 1871, application was made to the Congress of 1871-'72 for an appropriation of $100,000 for the purchase of a new site and the erection of suitable buildings thereon. Congress made the appropriation asked for, though the act was not passed until the 15th of May.

The board of trustees lost no time, after obtaining the new site, n contracting for the erection of a main building and a family building, plans of which were made by Edward Clark, Architect of the Capitol, and approved by the Secretary of the Interior.

The present site of the institution, old Fort Lincoln, is now called "Mount Lincoln," being an elevation overlooking the surrounding country for many miles distant. It is situated on the old Bladensburg turnpike-road, three miles east of the Capitol. The buildings now erected on this high point of land are conspicuous marks to a wide extent of country from every point of the compass. The site consists of one hundred and fifty acres of land, which is susceptible of great ornamental improvement. It was not selected till about the 20th of July.

The main building consists of a front extension, which is four stories high, with a spacious hall through the same. On the first floor are located the offices, reception-room, and officers' dining-rooms, and board-rooms. The second floor has the parlors, superintendent's living-apartment, one guest-chamber, and private office. The third floor is occupied by the officers of one of the families and guest-chambers. On the fourth floor are the store-rooms for clothing, &c., and bed-chambers for the house employés.

Two commodious wings extend from either side of the main building, said wings being each three stories high. The first floors of each are designed for dining-rooms, which will accommodate three hundred boys. One of these rooms is now occupied as a school-room temporarily. The second floor of this wing is used as a work-shop, and the same floor of the other wing is designed for a chapel. The third floors are used as dormitories for one family of boys that have to be quartered there now. When more family buildings are erected these floors will be used as reading-rooms, library-rooms, and tailor-shop. The building has all modern conveniences, is heated by steam throughout, and is well lighted by gas, and splendidly ventilated. There is a basement under the entire building, in which are located the kitchen, furnace-rooms, fuel and store-rooms, and several capacious cellars. There is a tower carried above the front extension of the building where an excellent view of the surrounding country can be had. A tank has been placed on the fourth floor of the main building, which is constantly supplied with good water forced above by steam-pumps from wells located near by.

The family building has a front projection, and is three stories high above the basement. The basement contains a furnace-room and large wash-room, and is also used for a play-room in wet and stormy weather. On the first floor are two rooms for the elder brother and his family, and a large school-room. The school-room is also used as a boys' sitting-room and for evening and devotional exercises. The second story contains rooms in the front extension for the assistant officer, and the main floor is a boys' dormitory, and a back projection furnishes the boys an entrance to the same, and also a room for a night-closet. The third floor is used for dormitory purposes, and the front rooms are used for storage, and one room is set apart for the boys' Sunday clothing. This building is plain but neatly finished and furnished, and makes a very comfortable and pleasant home for a family of fifty boys and the officers in charge of the same. The other buildings are such as were found on the farm when it was purchased, and while they are being utilized in the best possible way, it must be said that they do not serve in any comfortable degree the purposes for which they are used.

Bars, bolts, and walls are of no use here, and fences are needed only to keep the outer world from intruding, and not to restrain the boys or prevent escapes, for kind treatment is appreciated, and the sympathizing efforts and judicious management are incentives that so gain the higher nature of the boys, that the majority of them can at all times be trusted to go anywhere on the farm, and even to the city, without being attended by any one, and without any danger of their escaping.

Work-shops, more family buildings, and a good barn, and more officers are needed. The importance of juvenile reform institutions consists in the means of educating a class of youth whose education in everything that qualifies their future usefulness would otherwise be almost wholly neglected. It has been well said, "If society and individuals do not tax themselves for the *virtue* of the youth, they will be doubly taxed for the *vice* of the adult."

LIST OF TRUSTEES SINCE THE ORGANIZATION OF THE SCHOOL, AND THE DATE OF THEIR ORIGINAL APPOINTMENTS.

P. D. Gurley..Oct. 15, 1866.
William B. Webb ....Oct. 15, 1866.
George S. Gideon ....Oct. 15, 1866.
H. D. Cooke..Oct. 15, 1866.
B. F. Wiggett ....Oct. 15, 1866.
D. K. Cartter..Oct. 15, 1866.
S. J. Bowen ....Oct. 15, 1866.
Richard Wallach ....Oct. 15, 1867.
H. A. Brewster ....July 13, 1869.
N. Sargent ....Sept. 8, 1869.
D. V. Burr ....Sept. 24, 1869.
W. B. Todd..Oct. 15, 1869.
N. W. Burchell ....Oct. 15, 1870.
D. L. Eaton ....Oct. 15, 1870.
J. E. Carpenter......................................Oct. 15, 1871.
John Bailey ....Mar. 15, 1873.
H. A. Willard ....Feb. 12, 1875.
A. J. Falls ....Feb. 12, 1875.
Richard Joseph ....Apr. 7, 1876.
J. E. Fitch ....Aug. 4, 1876.

www.ingramcontent.com/pod-product-compliance
Lightning Source LLC
Chambersburg PA
CBHW081454070426
42452CB00042B/2731